Date:

(5)

A A a

A A A A A A A

A A A A A A A

A A A A A A A

A A A A A A A

A A A A A A A

a a a a a a a

a a a a a a a

a a a a a a a

a a a a a a a

a a a a a a a

HuSam Trace & Print:LETTERS, WORDS, SENTENCES (uppercase & lowercase)

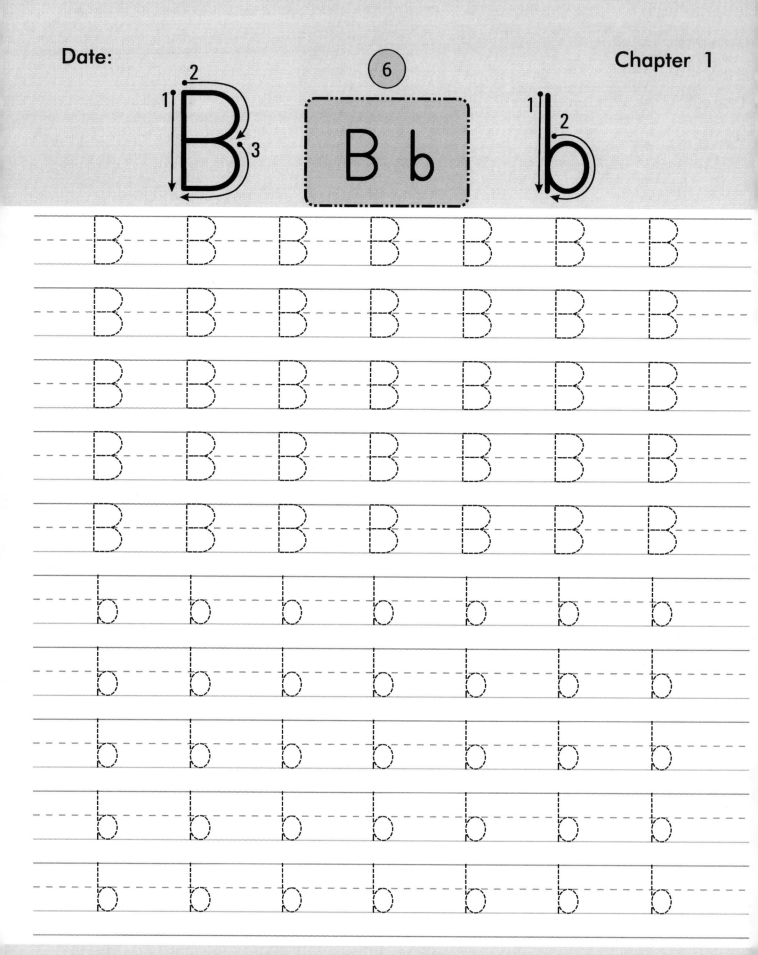

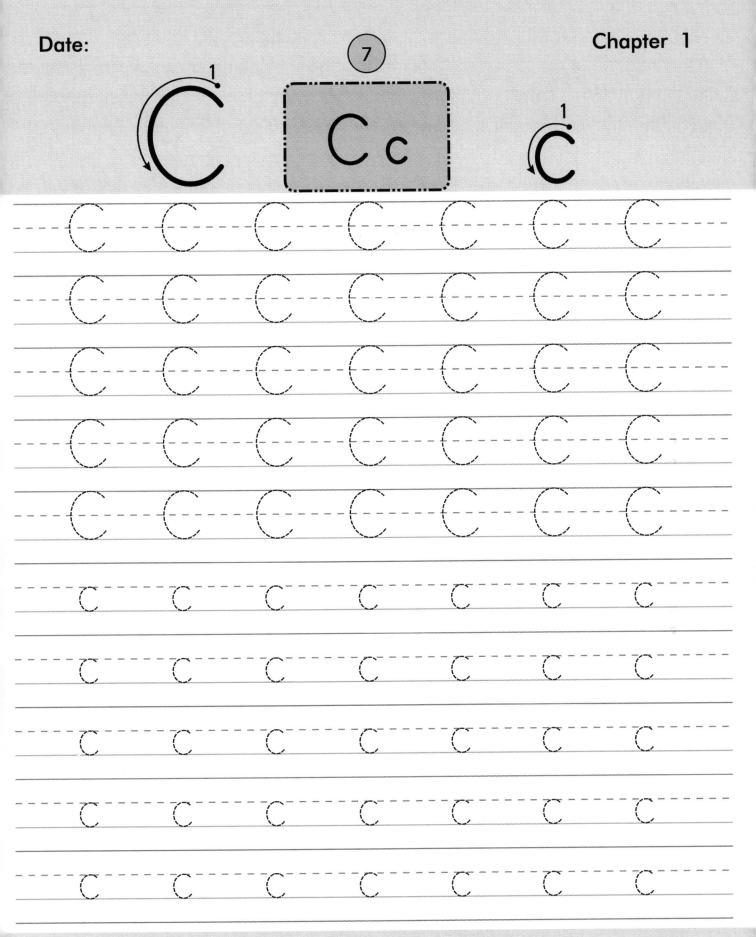

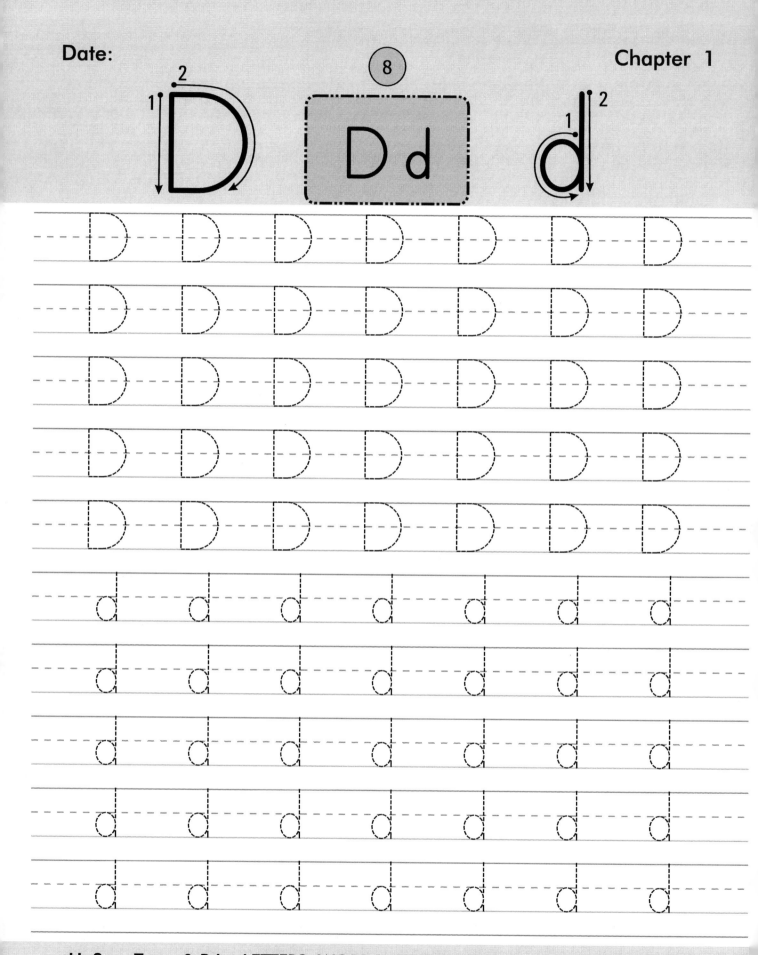

HuSam Trace & Print:LETTERS, WORDS, SENTENCES (uppercase & lowercase)

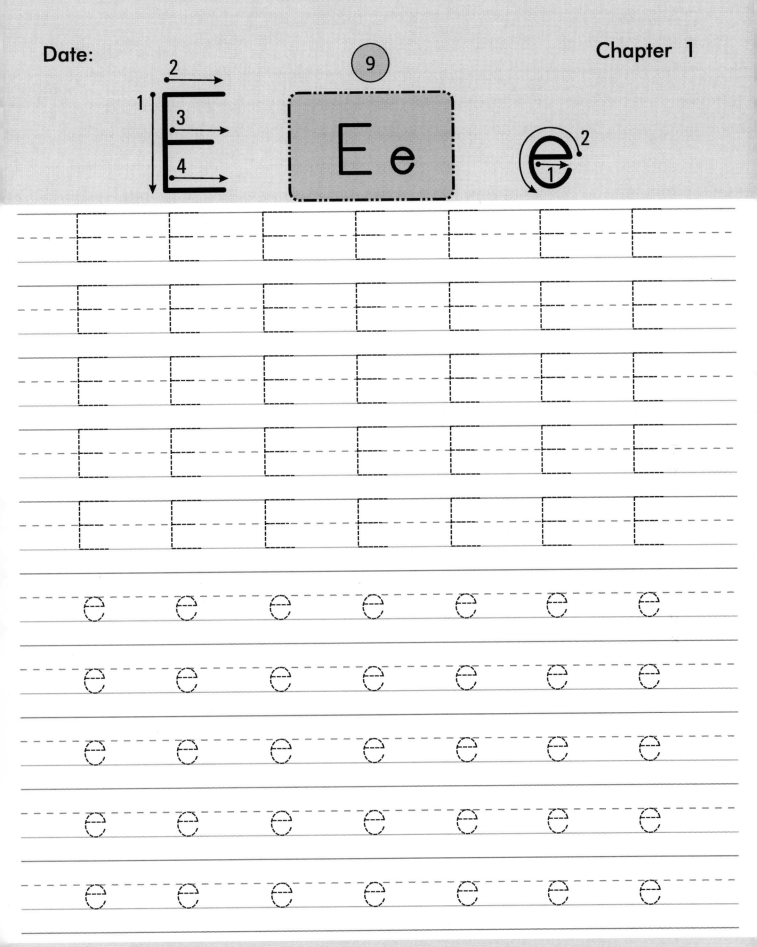

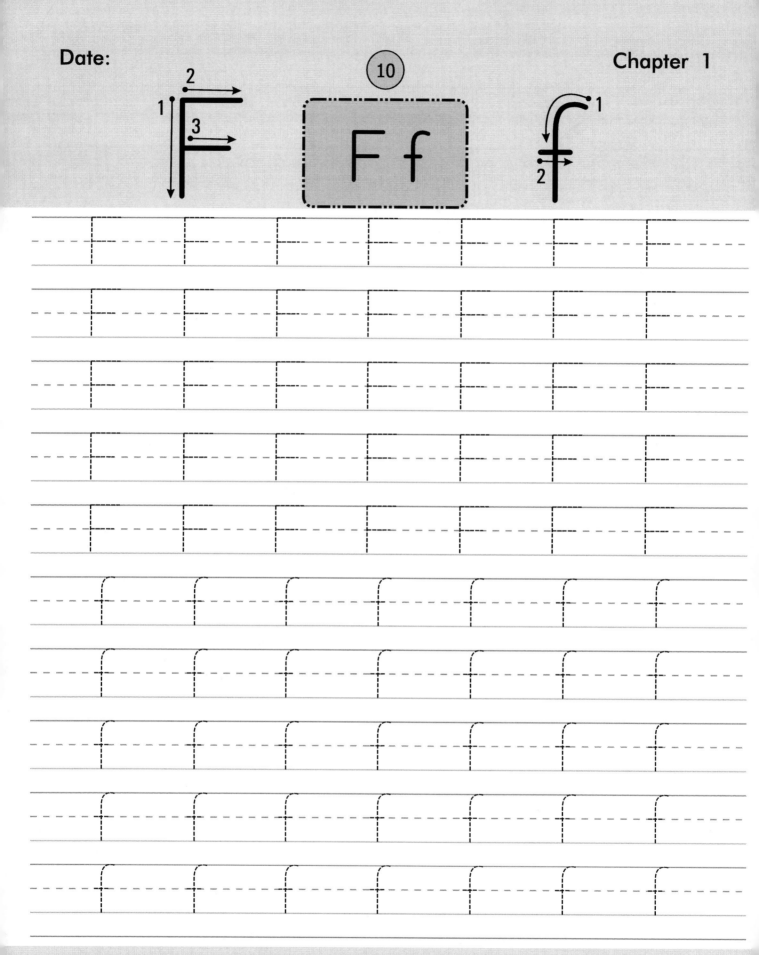

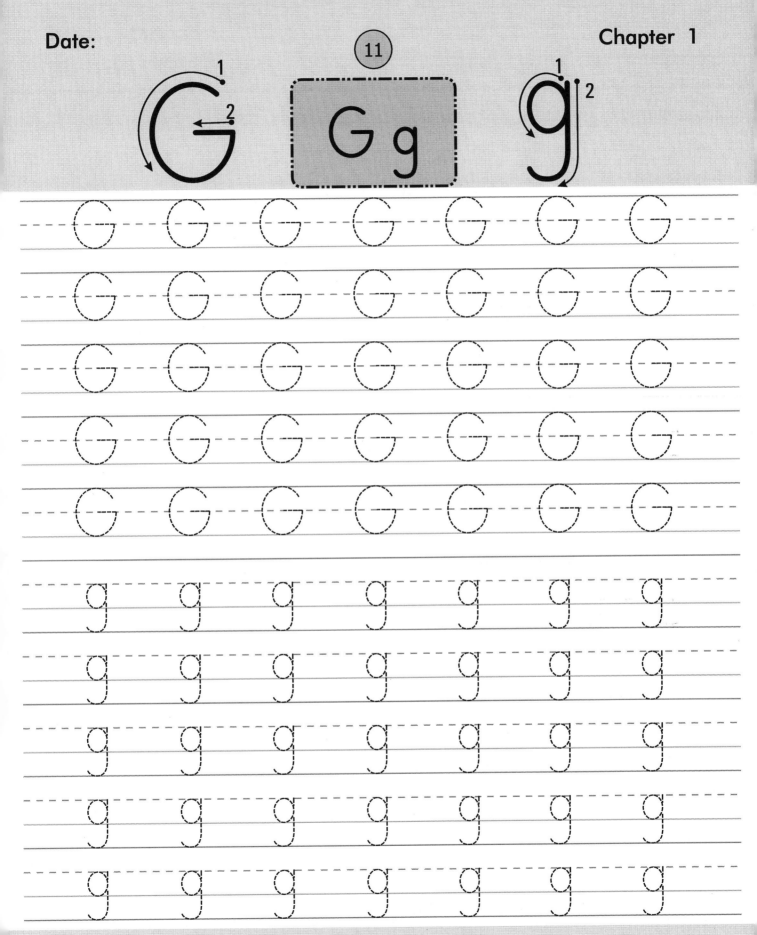

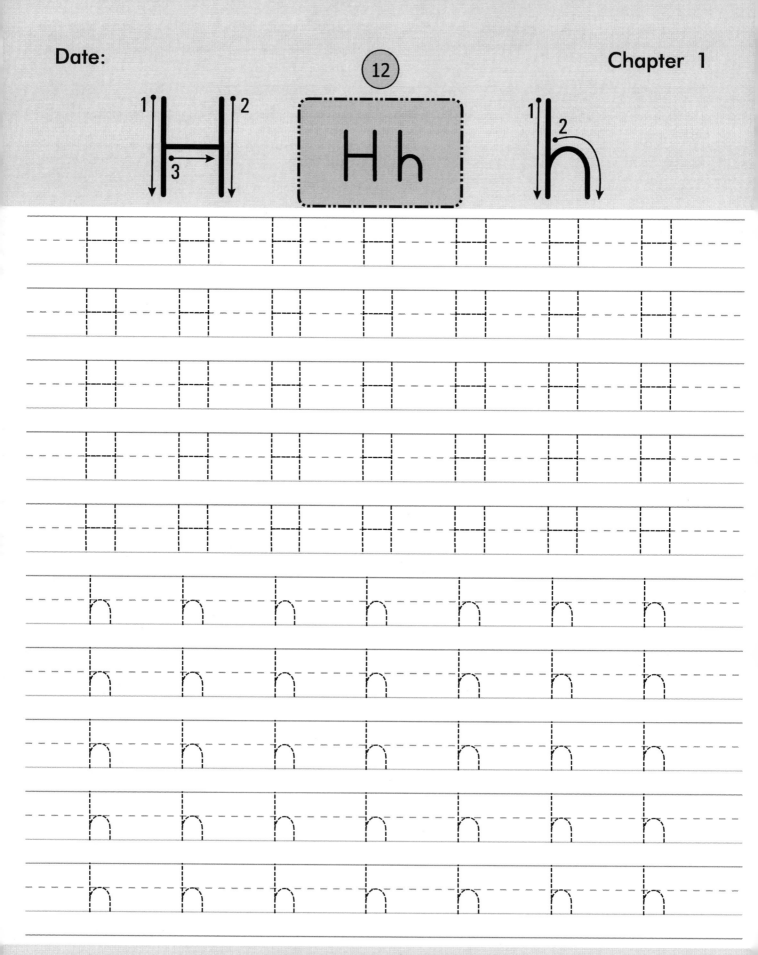

HuSam Trace & Print:LETTERS, WORDS, SENTENCES (uppercase & lowercase)

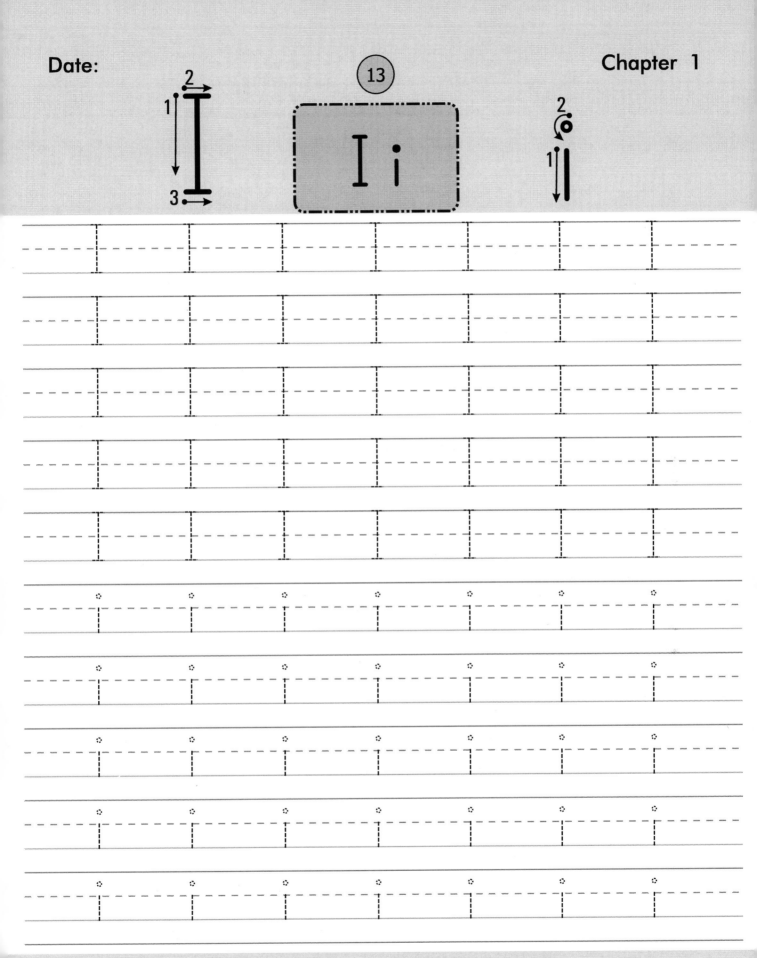

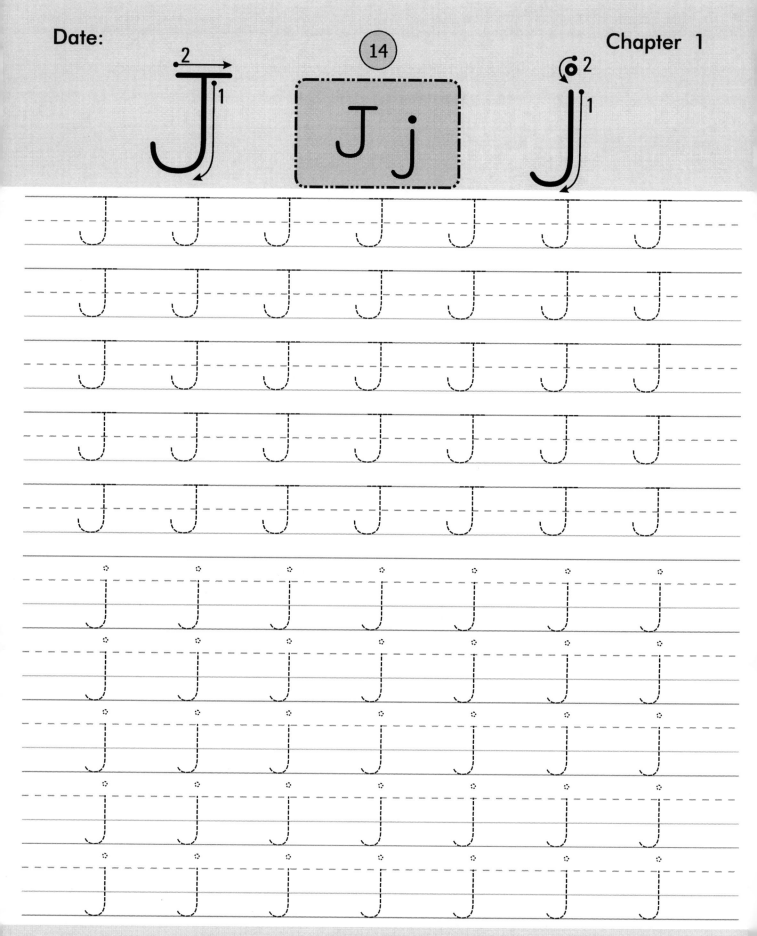

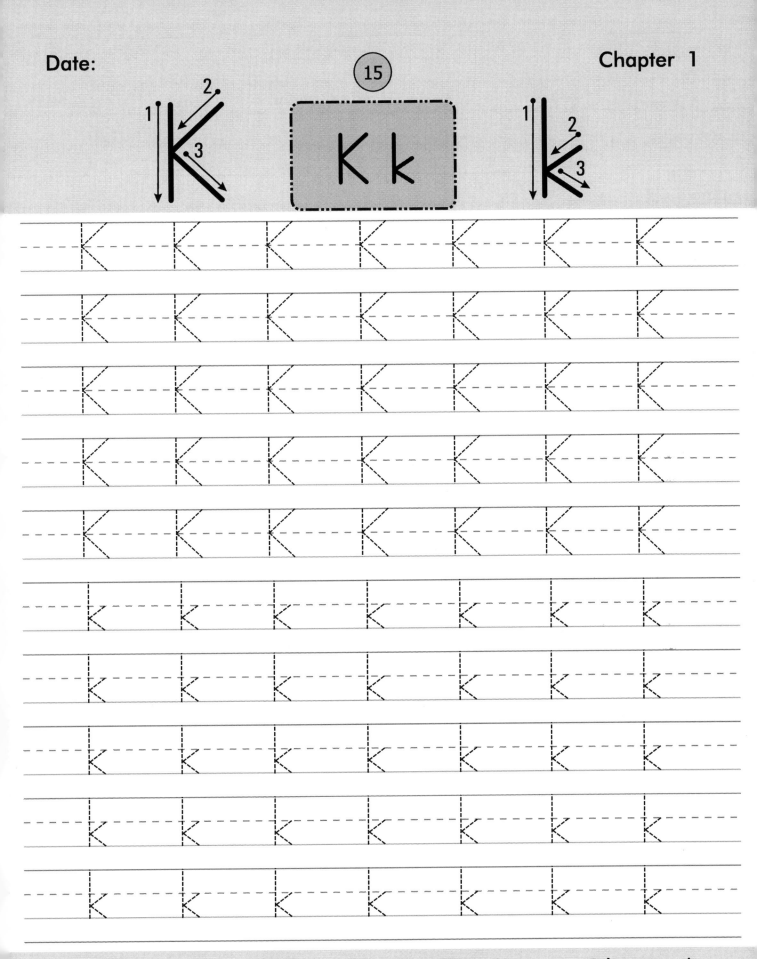

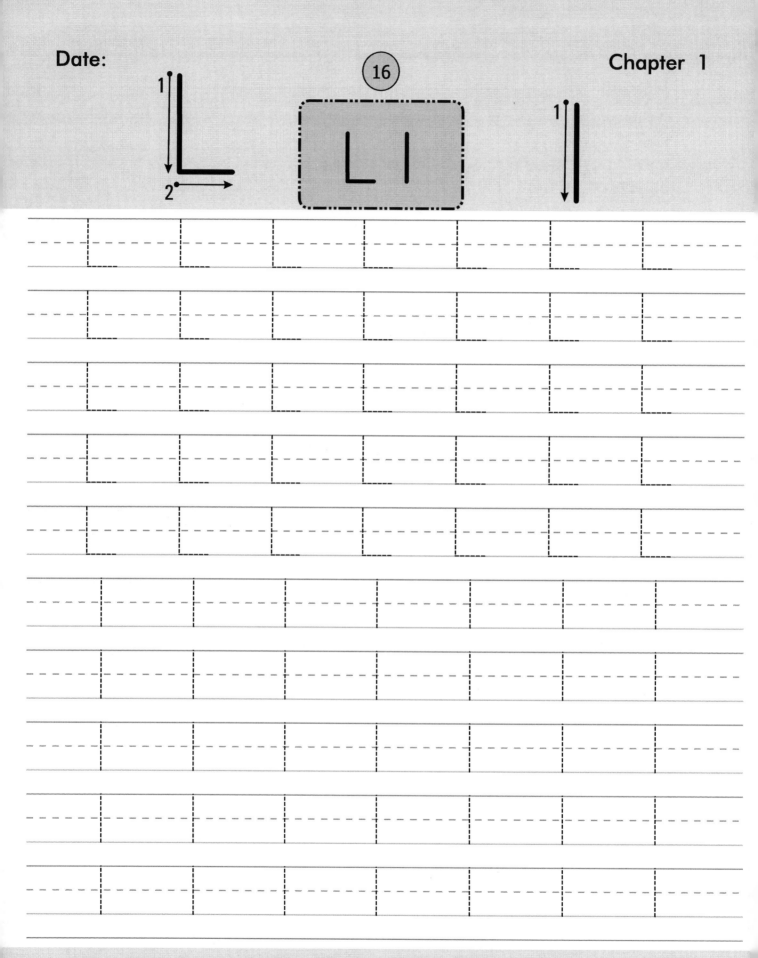

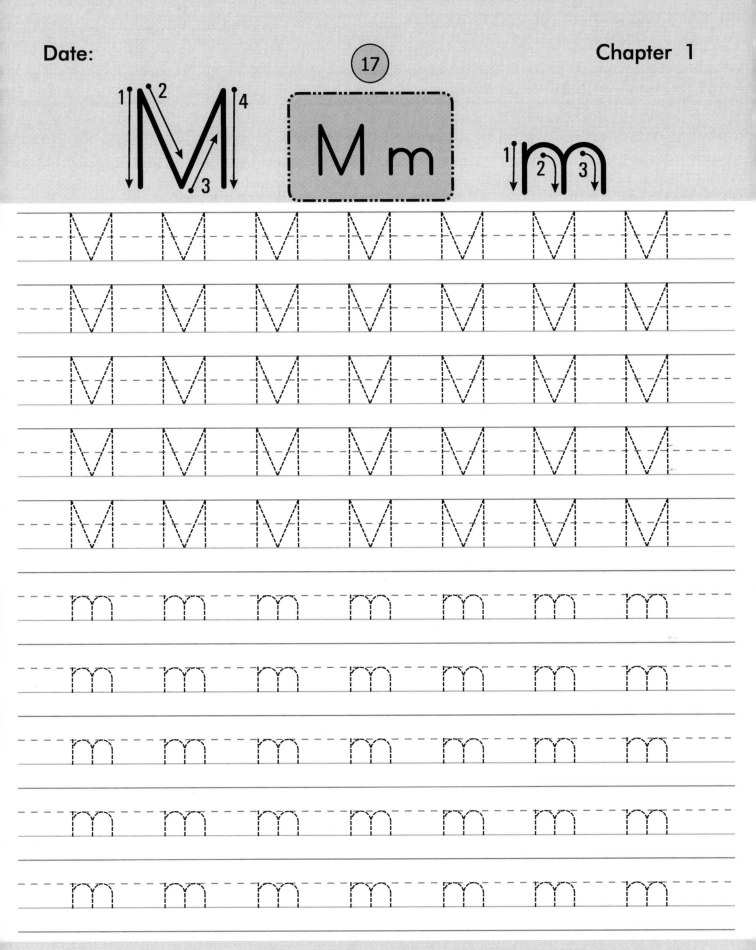

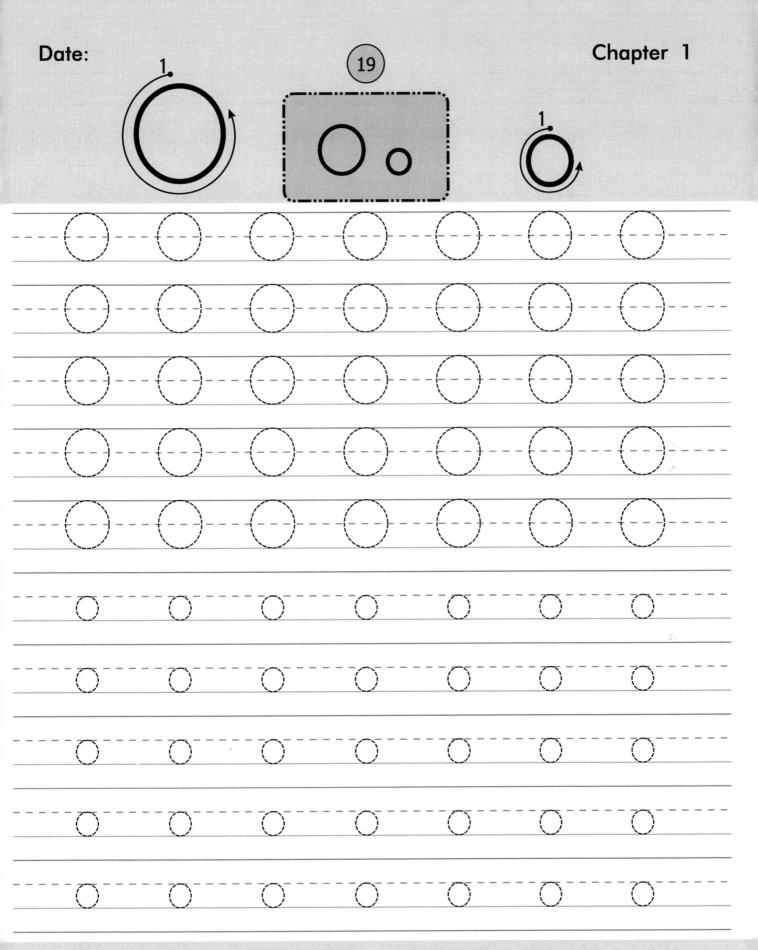

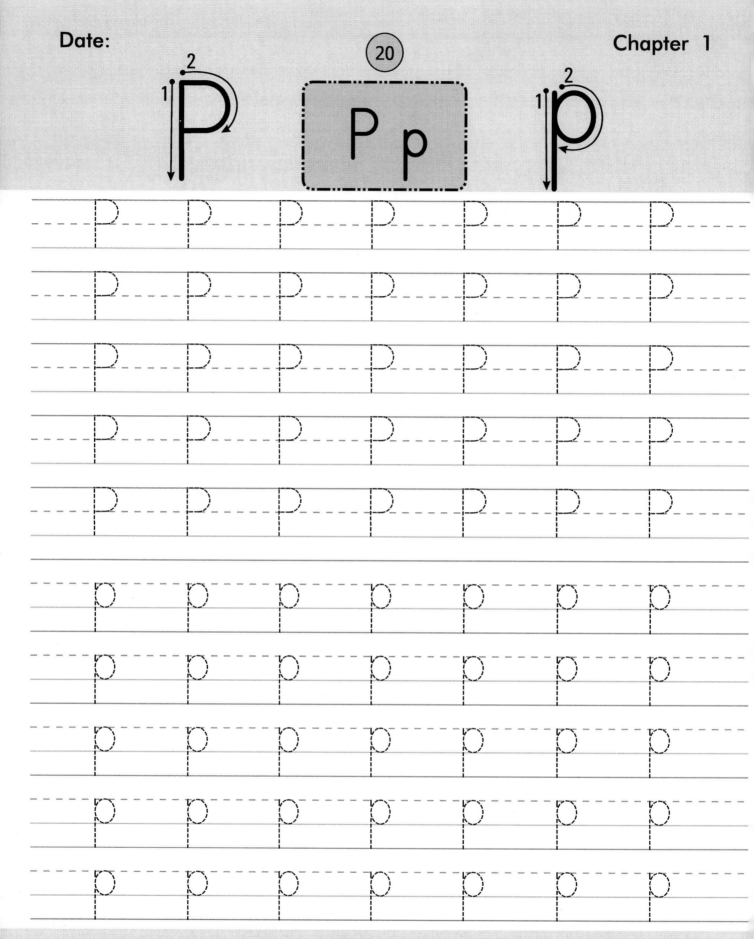

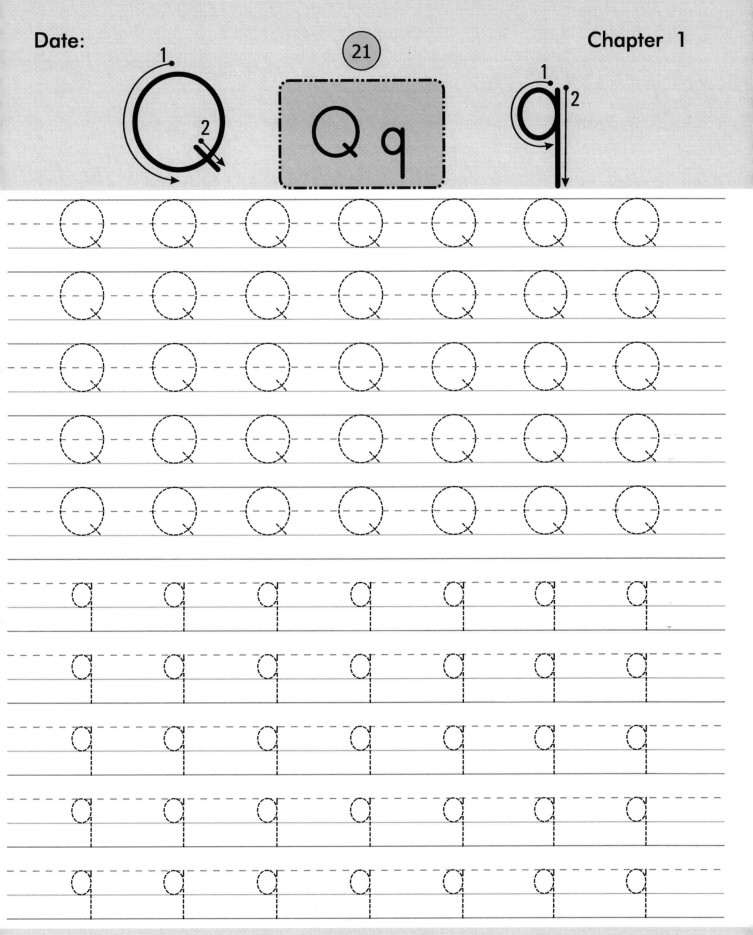

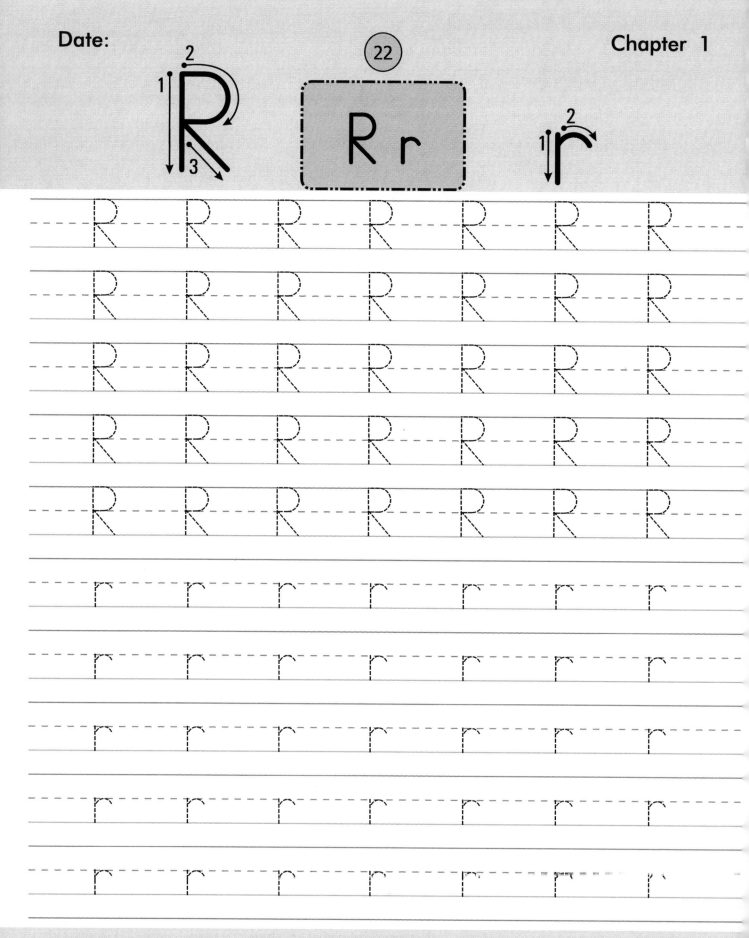

S S s

S S S S S S S

S S S S S S S

S S S S S S S

S S S S S S S

S S S S S S S

S S S S S S S

S S S S S S S

S S S S S S S

S S S S S S S

HuSam Trace & Print: LETTERS, WORDS, SENTENCES (uppercase & lowercase)

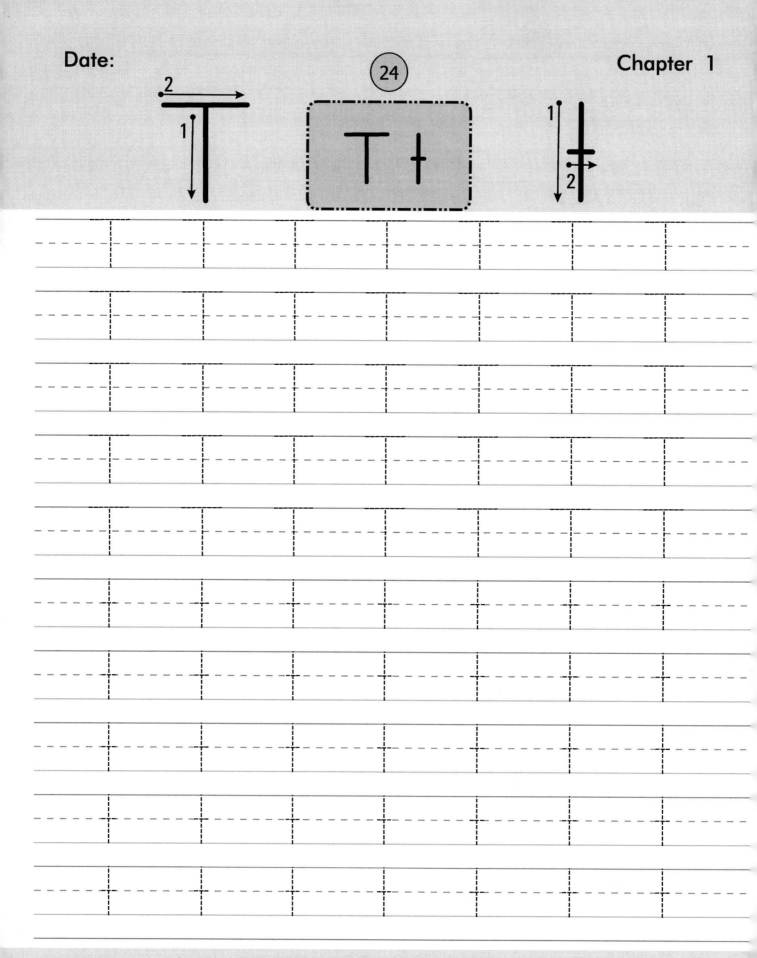

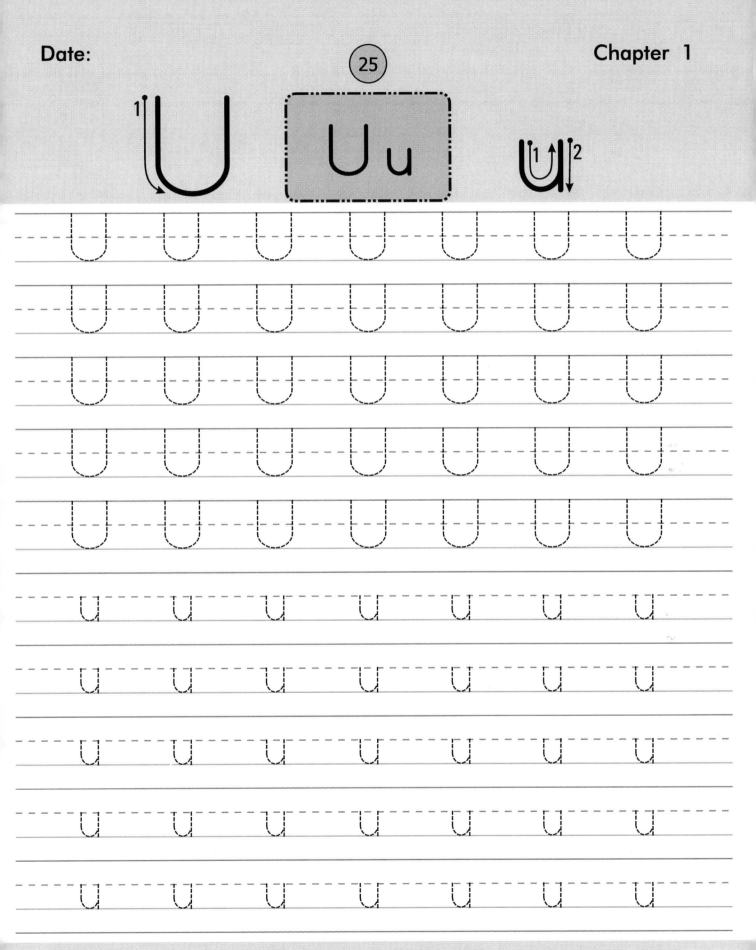

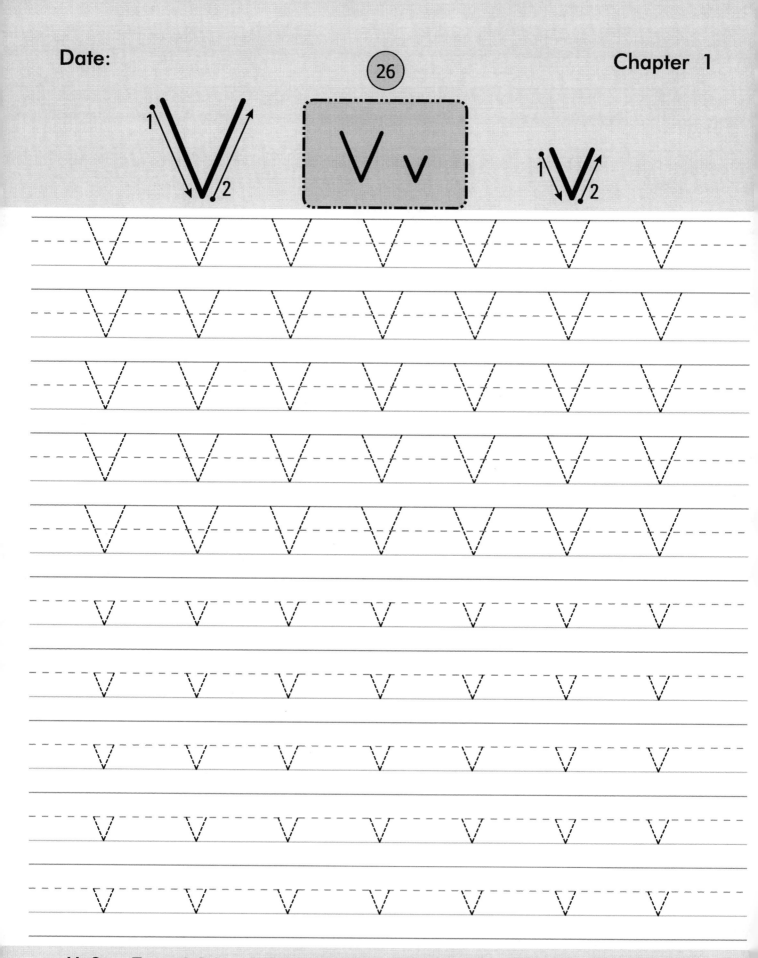

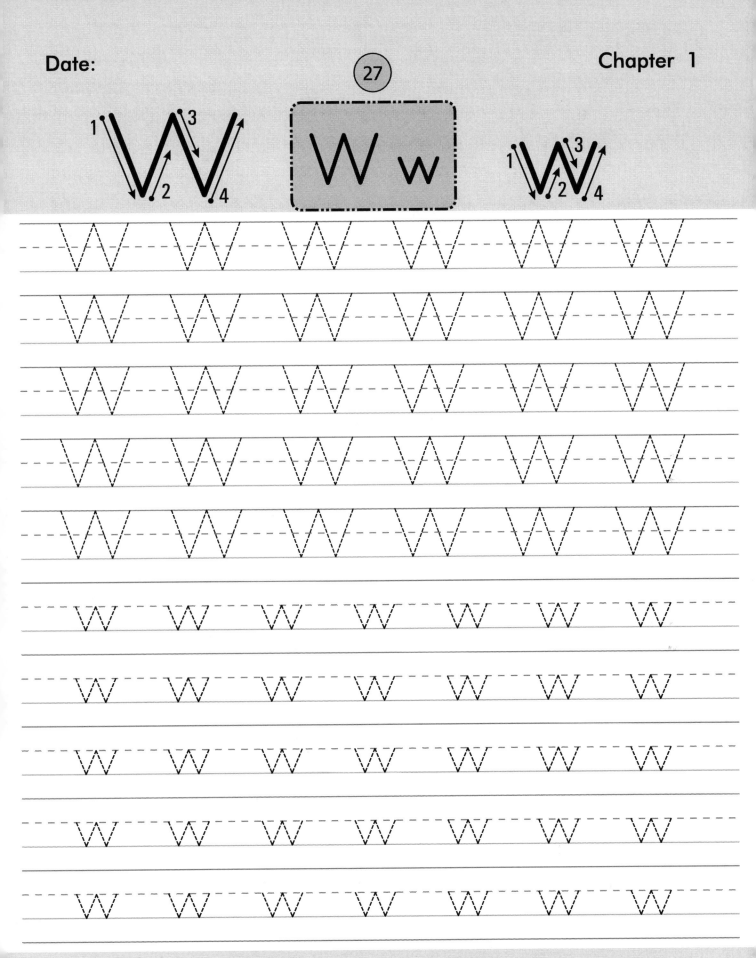

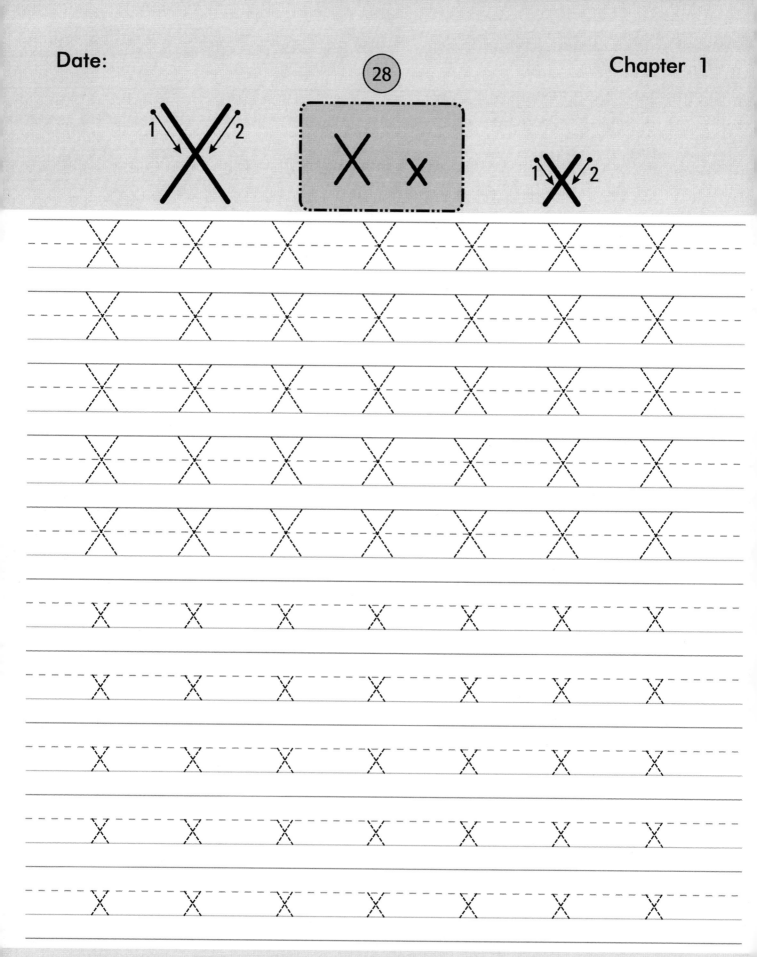

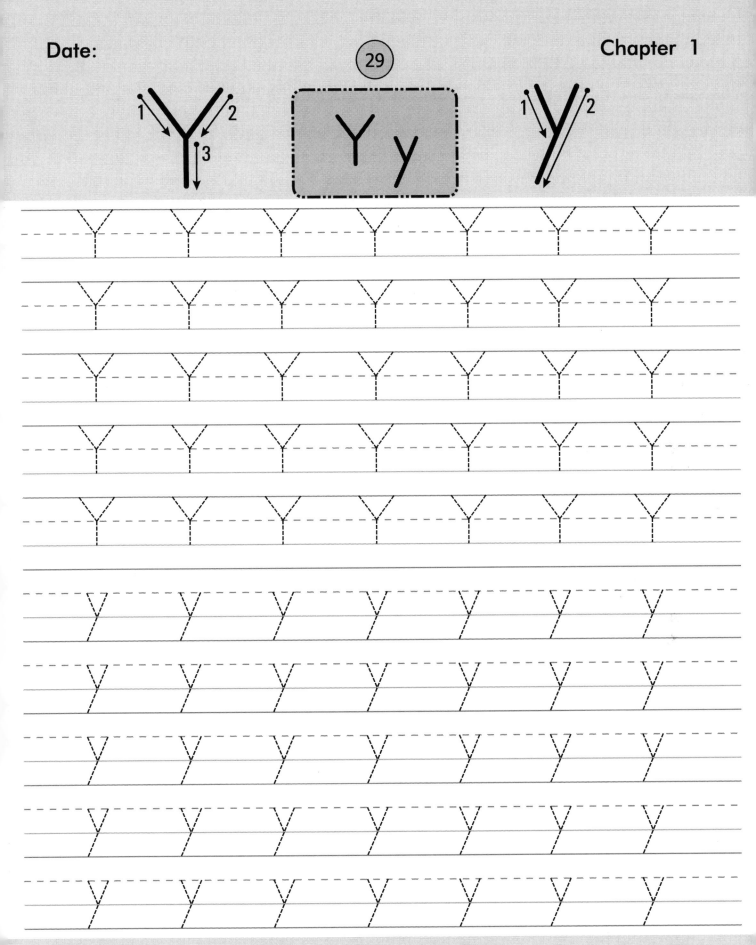

HuSam Trace & Print:LETTERS, WORDS, SENTENCES (uppercase & lowercase)

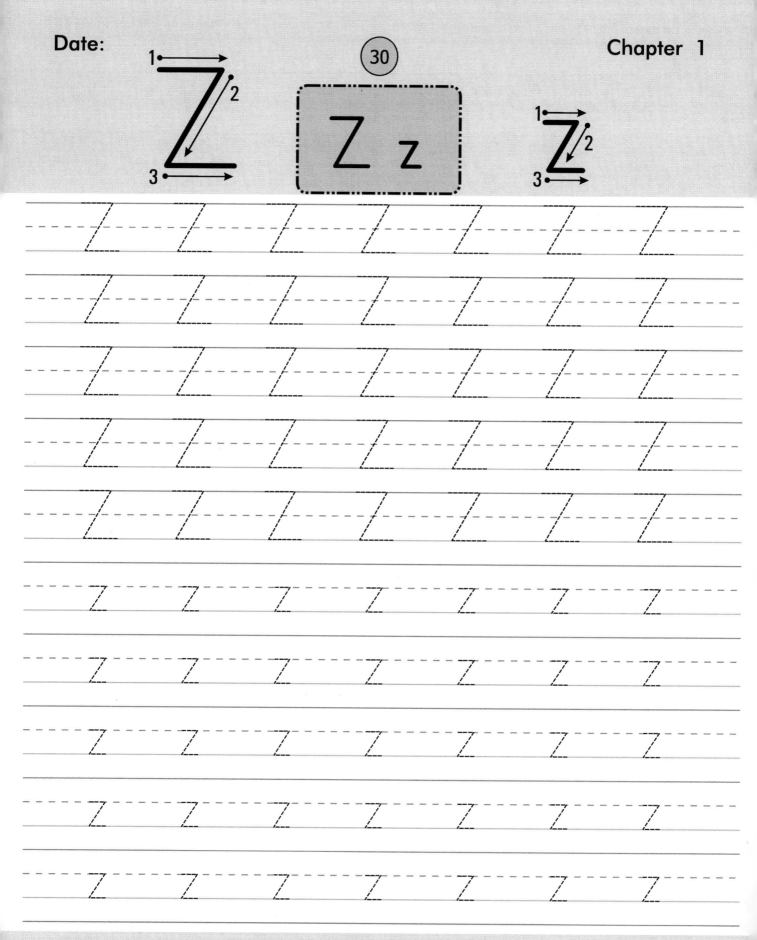

AFTER	A a	AGAIN
after		again

AFTER   AGAIN

AFTER   AGAIN

AFTER   AGAIN

after   again

after   again

after   again

HuSam Trace & Print:LETTERS, WORDS, SENTENCES (uppercase & lowercase)

BEFORE
before

B b

BREAD
bread

BEFORE   BREAD

BEFORE   BREAD

BEFORE   BREAD

before   bread

before   bread

before   bread

| CAMP camp | C c | CORNER corner |

CAMP   CORNER

CAMP   CORNER

CAMP   CORNER

camp   corner

camp   corner

camp   corner

DARK
dark

D d

DESERT
desert

DARK   DESERT

DARK   DESERT

DARK   DESERT

dark   desert

dark   desert

dark   desert

ELBOW
elbow

E e

EMPTY
empty

ELBOW   EMPTY

ELBOW   EMPTY

ELBOW   EMPTY

elbow   empty

elbow   empty

elbow   empty

FAIL fail	F f	FEVER fever

FAIL   FEVER

FAIL   FEVER

FAIL   FEVER

fail   fever

fail   fever

fail   fever

GLOVE
glove

G g

GIANT
giant

GLOVE   GIANT

GLOVE   GIANT

GLOVE   GIANT

glove   giant

glove   giant

glove   giant

HuSam Trace & Print:LETTERS, WORDS, SENTENCES (uppercase & lowercase)

HABIT
habit

Hh

HAMMER
hammer

HABIT   HAMMER

HABIT   HAMMER

HABIT   HAMMER

habit   hammer

habit   hammer

habit   hammer

HuSam Trace & Print: LETTERS, WORDS, SENTENCES (uppercase & lowercase)

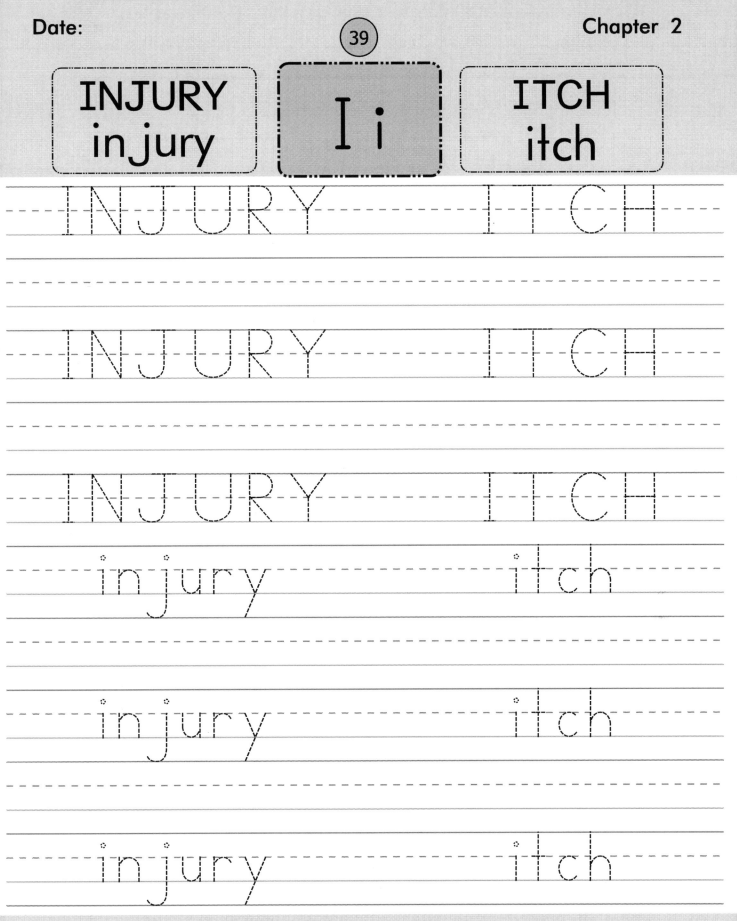

INJURY
injury

I i

ITCH
itch

JACKET
jacket

40

J j

JUDGE
judge

JACKET JUDGE

JACKET JUDGE

JACKET JUDGE

jacket judge

jacket judge

jacket judge

KNOCK	K k	KICK
knock		kick

KNOCK   KICK

KNOCK   KICK

KNOCK   KICK

knock   kick

knock   kick

knock   kick

LEMON
lemon

L l

LABEL
label

LEMON   LABEL

LEMON   LABEL

LEMON   LABEL

lemon   label

lemon   label

lemon   label

MARCH
march

M m

MONEY
money

MARCH MONEY

MARCH MONEY

MARCH MONEY

march money

march money

march money

NANNY
nanny

N n

NIECE
niece

NANNY   NIECE

NANNY   NIECE

NANNY   NIECE

nanny   niece

nanny   niece

nanny   niece

HuSam Trace & Print:LETTERS, WORDS, SENTENCES (uppercase & lowercase)

ORANGE
orange

O o

OVEN
oven

ORANGE   OVEN

ORANGE   OVEN

ORANGE   OVEN

orange   oven

orange   oven

orange   oven

| PHONE phone | **P p** | PAIN pain |

PHONE   PAIN

PHONE   PAIN

PHONE   PAIN

phone   pain

phone   pain

phone   pain

QUEEN
queen

Q q

QUICK
quick

QUEEN QUICK

QUEEN QUICK

QUEEN QUICK

queen quick

queen quick

queen quick

| REST
rest | R r | RAISE
raise |

REST   RAISE

REST   RAISE

REST   RAISE

rest   raise

rest   raise

rest   raise

| SMILE | S s | SECOND |
| smile | | second |

SMILE   SECOND

SMILE   SECOND

SMILE   SECOND

smile   second

smile   second

smile   second

TODAY
today

T t

TIME
time

TODAY TIME

TODAY TIME

TODAY TIME

today time

today time

today time

USEFUL
useful

U u

UNDER
under

USEFUL   UNDER

USEFUL   UNDER

USEFUL   UNDER

useful   under

useful   under

useful   under

| VIRUS | V v | VERY |
| virus | | very |

VIRUS   VERY

VIRUS   VERY

VIRUS   VERY

virus   very

virus   very

virus   very

WATCH
watch

W w

WAIT
wait

WATCH   WAIT

WATCH   WAIT

WATCH   WAIT

watch   wait

watch   wait

watch   wait

X-RAY
x-ray

X x

X-RAY
x-ray

X-RAY   X-RAY

X-RAY   X-RAY

X-RAY   X-RAY

x-ray   x-ray

x-ray   x-ray

x-ray   x-ray

| YEAR year | Y y | YELLOW yellow |

YEAR   YELLOW

YEAR   YELLOW

YEAR   YELLOW

year   yellow

year   yellow

year   yellow

ZIPPER
zipper

Z z

ZERO
zero

ZIPPER   ZERO

ZIPPER   ZERO

ZIPPER   ZERO

zipper   zero

zipper   zero

zipper   zero

MINUTE
minute

STAND
stand

MINUTE   STAND

MINUTE   STAND

MINUTE   STAND

minute   stand

minute   stand

minute   stand

EARTH
earth

DOCTOR
doctor

EARTH   DOCTOR

EARTH   DOCTOR

EARTH   DOCTOR

earth   doctor

earth   doctor

earth   doctor

INCOME
income

LITTLE
little

INCOME   LITTLE

INCOME   LITTLE

INCOME   LITTLE

income   little

income   little

income   little

POCKET
pocket

QUIET
quiet

POCKET   QUIET

POCKET   QUIET

POCKET   QUIET

pocket   quiet

pocket   quiet

pocket   quiet

SHADOW
shadow

TEST
test

SHADOW   TEST

SHADOW   TEST

SHADOW   TEST

shadow   test

shadow   test

shadow   test

WINDOW
window

YES
yes

WINDOW   YES

WINDOW   YES

WINDOW   YES

window   yes

window   yes

window   yes

**PICTURE
picture**

**KIND
kind**

PICTURE   KIND

PICTURE   KIND

PICTURE   KIND

picture   kind

picture   kind

picture   kind

HEALTH
health

FAMILY
family

HEALTH   FAMILY

HEALTH   FAMILY

HEALTH   FAMILY

health   family

health   family

health   family

ANKLE
ankle

GARAGE
garage

ANKLE   GARAGE

ANKLE   GARAGE

ANKLE   GARAGE

ankle   garage

ankle   garage

ankle   garage

JUICE
juice

LADDER
ladder

JUICE   LADDER

JUICE   LADDER

JUICE   LADDER

juice   ladder

juice   ladder

juice   ladder

POLICE
police

SCHOOL
school

POLICE SCHOOL

POLICE SCHOOL

POLICE SCHOOL

police school

police school

police school

KITCHEN
kitchen

DIRTY
dirty

KITCHEN   DIRTY

KITCHEN   DIRTY

KITCHEN   DIRTY

kitchen   dirty

kitchen   dirty

kitchen   dirty

COOKIE
cookie

OFFICE
office

COOKIE   OFFICE

COOKIE   OFFICE

COOKIE   OFFICE

cookie   office

cookie   office

cookie   office

WEAK
weak

FLOWER
flower

WEAK   FLOWER

WEAK   FLOWER

WEAK   FLOWER

weak   flower

weak   flower

weak   flower

READY
ready

DRESS
dress

READY   DRESS

READY   DRESS

READY   DRESS

ready   dress

ready   dress

ready   dress

HuSam Trace & Print: LETTERS, WORDS, SENTENCES (uppercase & lowercase)

MOUTH
mouth

STAMP
stamp

MOUTH   STAMP

MOUTH   STAMP

MOUTH   STAMP

mouth   stamp

mouth   stamp

mouth   stamp

| WOMAN | TOWN |
| woman | town |

WOMAN   TOWN

WOMAN   TOWN

WOMAN   TOWN

woman   town

woman   town

woman   town

CATCH
catch

FUNNY
funny

CATCH   FUNNY

CATCH   FUNNY

CATCH   FUNNY

catch   funny

catch   funny

catch   funny

DREAM
dream

ALARM
alarm

DREAM   ALARM

DREAM   ALARM

DREAM   ALARM

dream   alarm

dream   alarm

dream   alarm

FACTORY
factory

BANK
bank

FACTORY BANK

FACTORY BANK

FACTORY BANK

factory bank

factory bank

factory bank

HOLIDAY
holiday

KNOW
know

HOLIDAY   KNOW

HOLIDAY   KNOW

HOLIDAY   KNOW

holiday   know

holiday   know

holiday   know

MONTH
month

PEOPLE
people

MONTH PEOPLE

MONTH PEOPLE

MONTH PEOPLE

month people

month people

month people

WAX
wax

CREAM
cream

WAX   CREAM

WAX   CREAM

WAX   CREAM

wax   cream

wax   cream

wax   cream

CHAIR
chair

BLOCK
block

CHAIR   BLOCK

CHAIR   BLOCK

CHAIR   BLOCK

chair   block

chair   block

chair   block

EVENING
evening

ISLAND
island

EVENING   ISLAND

EVENING   ISLAND

EVENING   ISLAND

evening   island

evening   island

evening   island

REASON
reason

LINE
line

REASON　　　LINE

REASON　　　LINE

REASON　　　LINE

reason　　　line

reason　　　line

reason　　　line

The room is very cold.

The room is
very cold.

The room is
very cold.

The room is
very cold.

He is not in the kitchen.

He is not in

the kitchen.

He is not in

the kitchen.

He is not in

the kitchen.

Do you like these shoes?

Do you like
these shoes?

Do you like
these shoes?

Do you like
these shoes?

They want to talk to Dan.

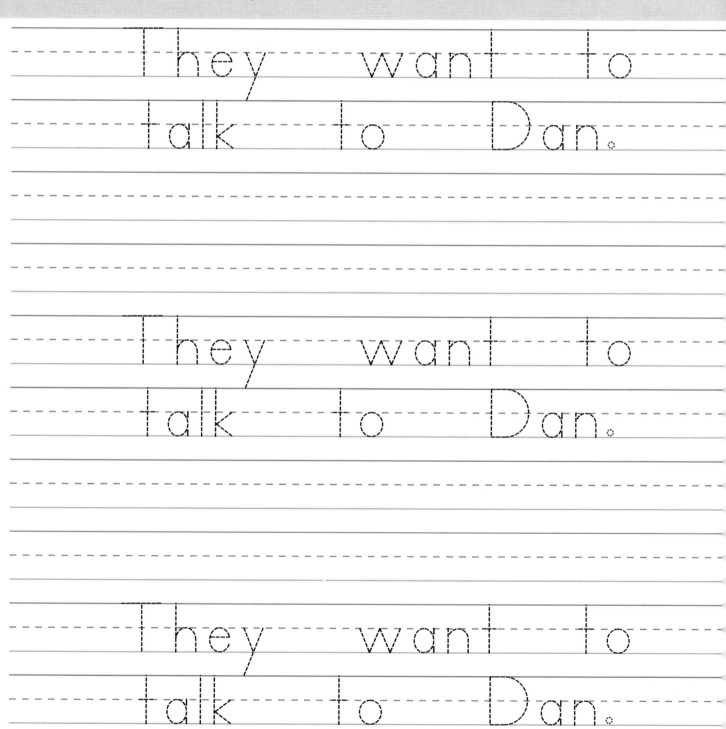

The ball is on the table.

The ball is on
the table.

The ball is on
the table.

The ball is on
the table.

She is looking at the clock.

She is looking
at the clock.

She is looking
at the clock.

She is looking
at the clock.

Give this book to my brother.

Give this book
to my brother.

Give this book
to my brother.

Give this book
to my brother.

He does not drink tea.

He does not

drink tea.

He does not

drink tea.

He does not

drink tea.

I thanked my friend again.

I thanked my
friend again.

I thanked my
friend again.

I thanked my
friend again.

I want to eat an orange.

I want to eat
an orange.

I want to eat
an orange.

I want to eat
an orange.

It was windy yesterday.

It was windy
yesterday.

It was windy
yesterday.

It was windy
yesterday.

We are going to school.

We are going
to school.

We are going
to school.

We are going
to school.

The birds will eat it.

The birds will
eat it.

The birds will
eat it.

The birds will
eat it.

It is not raining now.

It is not raining
now.

It is not raining
now.

It is not raining
now.

What are you doing there?

What are you
doing there?

What are you
doing there?

What are you
doing there?

I want to play here.

I want to play
here.

I want to play
here.

I want to play
here.

Please do not make any noise.

Please do not

make any noise.

Please do not

make any noise.

Please do not

make any noise.

They will be here soon.

They will be
here soon.

They will be
here soon.

They will be
here soon.

He needs two black pens.

He needs two

black pens.

He needs two

black pens.

He needs two

black pens.

Where is my blue shirt?

Where is my
blue shirt?

Where is my
blue shirt?

Where is my
blue shirt?

I was in class yesterday.

I was in class
yesterday.

I was in class
yesterday.

I was in class
yesterday.

I wake at six in the morning.

I wake at six

in the morning.

I wake at six

in the morning.

I wake at six

in the morning.

He kicked the ball to me.

He kicked the

ball to me.

He kicked the

ball to me.

He kicked the

ball to me.

I gave the keys to her.

I gave the keys
to her.

I gave the keys
to her.

I gave the keys
to her.

The boy was not at home.

The boy was
not at home.

The boy was
not at home.

The boy was
not at home.

This red box is empty.

This red box
is empty.

This red box
is empty.

This red box
is empty.

HuSam Trace & Print: LETTERS, WORDS, SENTENCES (uppercase & lowercase)

Made in the USA
Lexington, KY
30 September 2018